TOP 10 AFRICAN AMERICAN ATHLETES

BY K. C. KELLEY

Published by The Child's World®
1980 Lookout Drive • Mankato, MN 56003-1705
800-599-READ • www.childsworld.com

Photo credits:
AP: 6; Michael Probst 7; Jacob Harris 10; 12; Mark Duncan 15; 18, 19. Dreamstime.com: Samrat35 21. Library of Congress: 11. Newscom: Daryl Dennis/Icon SMI 8; Icon Sports Media 9; Adam Davis/Icon Sportswire 13; Brian Drake/SportsChrome 14; John Cordes/Icon Sportswire 16; Cynthia Lum/Icon Sportswire 17.

ISBN: 9781503827189
LCCN: 2017960459

Printed in the United States of America
PA02380

CONTENTS

INTRODUCTION

WHO'S NUMBER ONE?

African Americans have not been treated fairly in American history, and sports are no different. Sports are supposed to be about who can compete best on the day and win, fair and square. In some cases, black athletes have not been given the chance to show what they could do. For many of the athletes in this book, that was the case. Others, though, were able to achieve greatness, thanks to those who broke barriers.

Deciding which of these great people was the greatest is hard. There is no right answer. It's all up to you! What is your opinion? This book will help you decide.

Opinions are different than facts. Facts are real things. Michael Jordan won six NBA titles. That's a fact. Baseball is the greatest sport in the world. That's an opinion.

A tennis court is 78 feet (23.7 m) long. That's a fact. Wimbledon in England is the best place to watch tennis. That's an opinion. Some people might think baseball is not that great. But that's fine; that's their opinion. However, they can't say Jordan didn't win those championships. That's a fact.

And that's where *you* come in. You get to choose who is the greatest African American superstar ever. You will read lots of facts and stories about them. Based on that, what's your opinion? Who's No. 1? There are no wrong answers . . . but you might have some fun discussions with your sports-loving pals!

Read on, and then after you're done, make up your own Top 10 list.

Lisa Leslie

NUMBERS, NUMBERS

Pro Sports' First Season with African Americans

MLB	1947
NBA	1946
NFL	1946
NHL	1958

JIM BROWN

FOOTBALL • LACROSSE

Brown was a great all-around athlete. In college, he became one of the best lacrosse players ever.

Even more than 50 years after he played, Jim Brown is still considered one of the best running backs in NFL history. After he retired, he became a respected civil rights leader.

Brown joined the NFL's Cleveland Browns in 1957 and led the league in rushing yards and touchdowns. That was the first of nine NFL rushing titles he would win in his Hall of Fame career. He was the NFL MVP four times: 1957, 1958, 1963, and 1965. His career average of 104.3 yards (95 m) per game is the best in NFL history.

Brown surprised the NFL by retiring in 1965. He became an actor in many popular movies. He also spoke out loudly and often against racism.

NUMBERS, NUMBERS

Jim Brown Rushing Yards

Year	Yards
1957	942*
1958	1,527*
1959	1,329*
1960	1,257*
1961	1,408*
1962	996
1963	1,863*
1964	1,446*
1965	1,544*

** Led NFL*

JACKIE JOYNER-KERSEE

TRACK AND FIELD

Jackie Joyner-Kersee is probably the best all-around female athlete ever.

Growing up in St. Louis, she played track and field, basketball, and volleyball. Her best results came in the **heptathlon**. This two-day event includes seven contests in track and field. Only the best, most fit and talented athletes can do well.

At the 1988 Olympic Games, she set a heptathlon world record that still stands and won the gold medal. She also won the gold in the long jump. She won heptathlon gold in 1992, too.

In 2000, Joyner-Kersee was named the top woman athlete of the 20th century by several magazines and groups of experts.

The heptathlon has seven events, in this order: (first day) 100-meter hurdles, high jump, shot put, 200-meter run; (second day) long jump, javelin, 800-meter run.

NUMBERS, NUMBERS

Only three women have broken the 7,000-point level in the heptathlon. Joyner-Kersee is one of them and she did it SIX times!

LISA LESLIE

BASKETBALL

Leslie was the first woman ever to dunk in a pro game. She slammed home a basket in 2002.

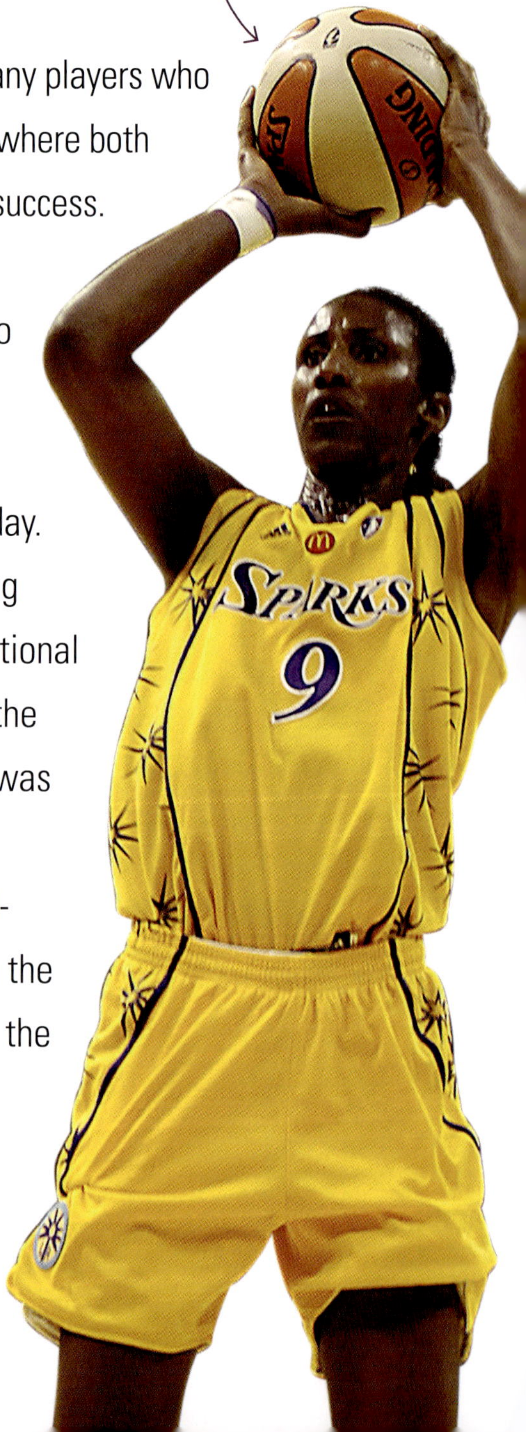

You might hear from hoops fans that there are many players who could fill this top 10 spot. Basketball is one sport where both women and African Americans have had a lot of success. But Lisa Leslie was a dominant player and also a pioneer. She was one of the first female players to really play with power and force. She helped the sport grow and become popular. Without her, the WNBA might not have become the big hit it is today.

In high school, she set a single-game scoring record with 101 points! At USC, she was the national player of the year as a senior. Then she helped the Los Angeles Sparks win two WNBA titles. She was WNBA MVP three times.

Leslie was also on four Olympic gold-medal-winning U.S. teams. In 2015, she was named to the Basketball Hall of Fame and has become one of the Sparks' co-owners.

NUMBERS, NUMBERS

Leslie never averaged less than 15 points per game in any of her 12 WNBA seasons.

CARL LEWIS

TRACK AND FIELD

In 1991, Lewis set a 100-meter world record with a time of 9.86 seconds.

Carl Lewis set a national high school record in the long jump . . . and just kept leaping! When he was done, he was one of the most successful track and field athletes of all time.

Lewis focused on the sprints and the long jump. Jesse Owens had won four Olympic gold medals in 1936. In 1984, Lewis matched that amazing record. Lewis won the 100 meters and 200 meters, plus was part of the winning 4x100-meter relay team. He won the long jump, too. What was most amazing was that he won while under the pressure of everyone expecting him to win. Champions come through when the spotlight is brightest.

He went on to win the long jump in four straight Olympic games, a feat matched by only one other track athlete. Lewis's career total was nine Olympic gold medals.

NUMBERS, NUMBERS

Lewis's Gold

1984: 100 meters, 200 meters, 4x100-meter relay, long jump

1988*: 100 meters, long jump

1992: 4x100-meter relay, long jump

1996: Long jump

** Also won 200-meter silver*

WILLIE MAYS

BASEBALL

In a 1961 game, Mays hit four homers. He was only the seventh player to do that in the 1900s. Through 2017, that total was up to only 15.

Few baseball players had as many all-around skills as this great outfielder. Known as the "Say-Hey Kid," Willie Mays hit for power, played amazing defense, and flew around the bases.

After a season in the **Negro Leagues**, Mays burst into the big leagues with the New York Giants. He was the 1951 Rookie of the Year. In 1954 he was MVP and helped the Giants win the World Series.

Mays was a feared slugger, with six seasons of 40 homers or more. His 660 career homers are fifth most. He is one of only two players with 300 steals and more than 500 homers.

Mays earned a second MVP award in 1965 when he was 34 years old. As of 2018, Mays is known as the greatest living baseball player.

NUMBERS, NUMBERS

League Leader

Mays was tops in the NL in many stat categories. Here are a few:

Stat	Times Led NL
Home Runs	4
Stolen Bases	4
Batting Average	1
Slugging Pct.	5
Runs	2

JESSE OWENS

TRACK AND FIELD

Jesse Owens ran straight out of poverty and into history. He was born on a farm in the **segregated** South. His parents were the children of slaves. Owens and his family moved to Ohio when he was nine. There he discovered he had a gift for running fast.

He went on become one of the few black students at Ohio State. Though he put up with injustices, he kept running. At the 1935 **Big Ten** championships that year, he set four world records (WR) in less than an hour!

The next year, he became a legend. The 1936 Olympics were held in Germany. That country was run by the racist Adolf Hitler and his Nazi Party. They believed black people were inferior to whites. Under great pressure, Owens stood up to the Nazis and dominated the Games. He won four gold medals in a powerful performance.

Owens was given the Presidential Medal of Freedom in 1976. This is America's highest civilian honor.

NUMBERS, NUMBERS

One Amazing Day

Here is what Owens did on May 25, 1935:

Time	Event	Result	
3:15	100 meters	9.4 seconds	WR (tie)
3:30	Long jump	26.825 inches	WR
3:39	220 yards	20.3 seconds	WR
4:00	200-yard hurdles	22.6	WR

JACKIE ROBINSON

BASEBALL

On April 15, 1947, fans at Ebbets Field in Brooklyn, New York, watched history. Many of those fans were African American, and they were especially thrilled. Playing first base for the Brooklyn Dodgers that day was Jackie Robinson. He became the first black player in the Major Leagues in the 20th century. It was one of the most important moments in American history.

Robinson grew up in California. In college at UCLA, he starred for four of its sports teams. After college, he entered the U.S. Army. The Army then was mostly segregated. Robinson was an officer, but he felt like he was treated as a second-class citizen. He got in trouble with white officers for speaking up.

After the Army, he joined the Negro Leagues' Kansas City Monarchs.

Every year on April 15, all Major Leaguers honor Robinson by wearing his uniform number 42, which is retired by all teams.

At the same time, Branch Rickey was trying to change baseball. He was the general manager of the Dodgers. He wanted to hire African Americans. But baseball had an unwritten rule against that. Rickey thought this was wrong. He asked Robinson if he would take on the challenge of being first. Rickey knew that many people would object. He told Robinson that the player could not fight back, he could not respond. Only by showing courage would this experiment succeed.

Robinson took on the job with pride. He wanted to play and he wanted other black athletes to join him. It was very hard at first. Some fans yelled awful words. Opponents tried to hit him with pitches or step on him with spiked shoes. But Robinson stuck it out. He not only played, he became a star, winning the 1947 Rookie of the Year award. Over the next decade, he helped the Dodgers reach the World Series six times. In 1955, they won their first World Series and all of Brooklyn cheered.

Robinson retired in 1956 and became a popular speaker about civil rights.

NUMBERS, NUMBERS

Robinson's Key Honors

1947 NL Rookie of the Year

1949 NL Most Valuable Player

6 All-Star Game selections

.342 batting average led NL, 1949

MICHAEL JORDAN

BASKETBALL

When he was most famous, a TV commercial said that people should try to "Be Like Mike!" That's just not possible. No one, and certainly no player, will ever be like Michael Jordan. On just about every list of "best basketball players ever," his name is at or near the top.

Jordan grew up in North Carolina. He was small in high school, but he grew and worked hard and played at the University of North Carolina. As a **freshman**, he hit the game-winning shot when his school won the national championship. Before he joined the NBA, he won a gold medal at the Summer Olympics. (He won a second gold in 1992.)

"MJ" joined the Chicago Bulls. He thrilled fans—and scared opponents—with his leaping ability.

Jordan led the NBA in scoring average 10 times, by far the most ever.

Jordan's scoring average of 30.12 points per game is the highest in NBA history. His 32,292 career points are fourth most all-time.

Jordan won the 1988 NBA Slam Dunk Contest with a soaring slam!

He led the NBA in scoring in 1987. He would repeat that feat nine more times, tying an all-time record. In 1991, he led the Bulls to their first NBA title. The team dominated the NBA, winning two more times.

Then Jordan shocked everyone by leaving the NBA to try baseball. He had recently lost his father and he wanted to try a sport they both loved. Jordan didn't do too well, and soon came back to the Bulls. He once again led the NBA in scoring and carried them to three more championships in a row.

Jordan retired again in 2003 and bought part of the Washington Wizards. He came back to play two seasons with that team before leaving the court for good. He co-owns the Charlotte Bobcats. He continues to have a big impact on the sport he loves, helping young players for his team improve. They won't ever be like Mike, but maybe they can get close!

NUMBERS, NUMBERS

MJ's Big Awards

MVP: 1988, 1991, 1992, 1996, 1998

NBA Finals MVP: 6

All-Star Game MVP: 3

SERENA WILLIAMS

TENNIS

Serena Williams is perhaps the greatest female athlete in history. She has dominated tennis and rewritten the record book. More importantly, she has done so in the face of haters and critics. She has stood tall and proud and become a role model for women and girls everywhere.

By the time she was eight, Serena was a superstar. When she was 14, Williams played her first pro match. Her sister Venus was also a young pro star. As Serena won more and more, she had to deal with some negative attention. Some fans and tennis people didn't like the way she played. She was too powerful, they said. What some people did not say out loud, though, was that they didn't like the black sisters being so good.

Venus Williams is a superstar player, too. She has won seven Grand Slam singles titles. Teaming with Serena, they have won 14 Grand Slam doubles championships.

Tennis was played mostly by white people and the sisters were something new. They were not the first black players, but they were certainly the most successful.

Through it all, Serena's talent shined. Together with Venus, the Williams sisters changed tennis. In 1999, Serena was the first African American woman since 1958 to win the U.S. Open. In 2003, she won the Australian Open for the first time. That gave her titles in all four of the **Grand Slam** events.

In 2002–2003, Serena won the four Grand Slam events in a row. She repeated the feat from 2014-2015. The streaks became known as Serena Slams. Pairing up with Venus, Serena also won Olympic gold medals in doubles in 2000, 2008, and 2012. In 2017, she set a new record for Grand Slam singles wins with 23.

NUMBERS, NUMBERS

Serena's Grand Slams	
Australian Open	7
French Open	3
US Open	6
Wimbledon	7

MUHAMMAD ALI

BOXING

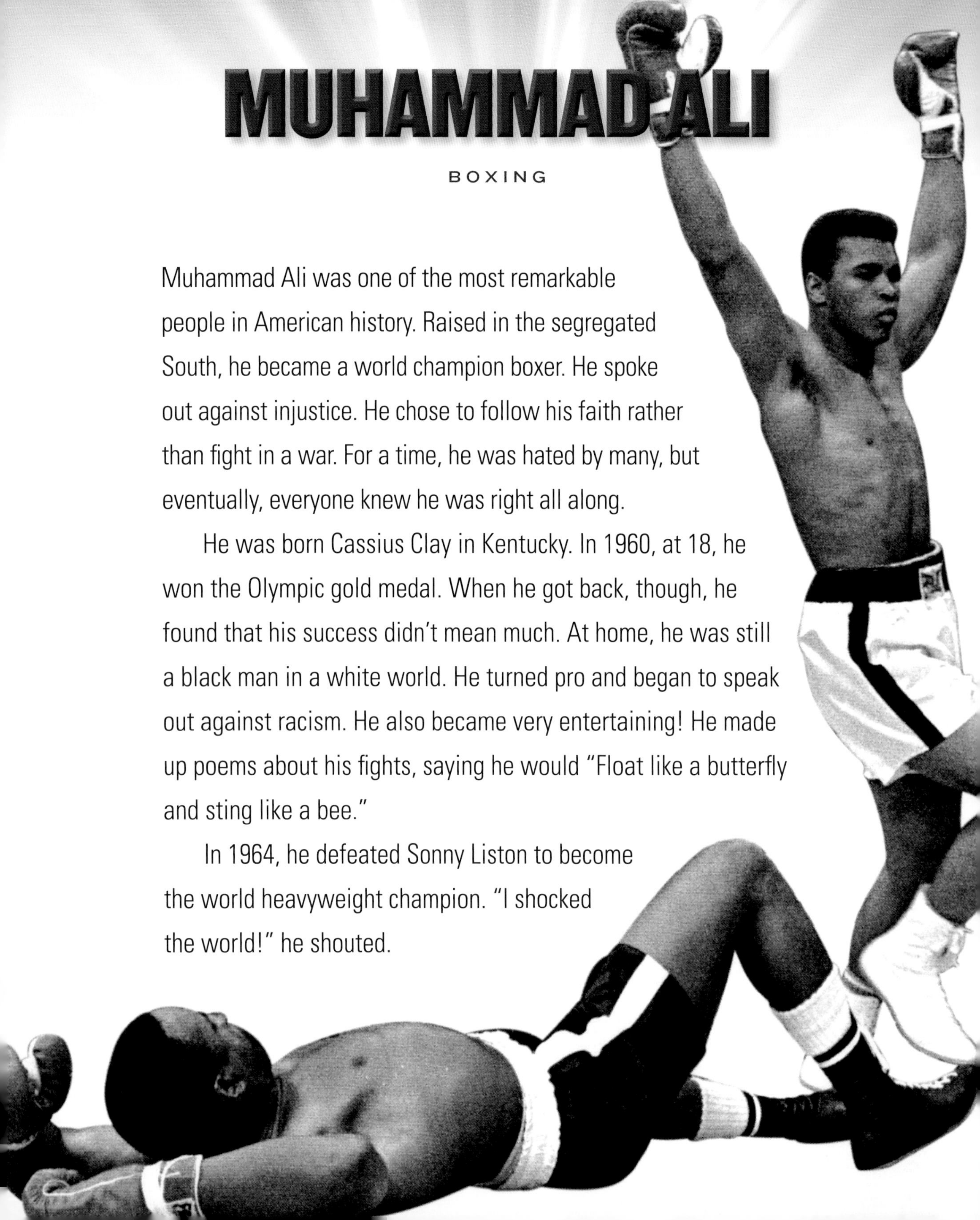

Muhammad Ali was one of the most remarkable people in American history. Raised in the segregated South, he became a world champion boxer. He spoke out against injustice. He chose to follow his faith rather than fight in a war. For a time, he was hated by many, but eventually, everyone knew he was right all along.

He was born Cassius Clay in Kentucky. In 1960, at 18, he won the Olympic gold medal. When he got back, though, he found that his success didn't mean much. At home, he was still a black man in a white world. He turned pro and began to speak out against racism. He also became very entertaining! He made up poems about his fights, saying he would "Float like a butterfly and sting like a bee."

In 1964, he defeated Sonny Liston to become the world heavyweight champion. "I shocked the world!" he shouted.

In 1978, Ali became the first boxer to win the heavyweight title three times. He defeated Leon Spinks, who had beaten him earlier that year.

Then he gave it another shock. Soon after the fight, he announced that he was changing his name to Muhammad Ali. He was following the religion of Islam. This made many fans very unhappy. Sports writers refused to use his new name.

In 1967, he was called to serve in the U.S. Army. He refused. He said his faith did not allow him to go to war. His actions were against the law. He was not allowed to box for more than three years. Finally, the courts ruled in his favor. He began to box again. He fought Joe Frazier three times, winning two of these huge events. By the mid-1970s, Ali was the most famous person in the world. Eventually, all the boxing took its toll. He finally retired in 1978. Soon after, doctors said he had **Parkinson's disease**. It would take away his power of speech. It made it hard for him to move. Still, he traveled the world trying to bring peace. The world **mourned** when he died in 2016.

NUMBERS, NUMBERS

Ali's Boxing Stats

Fights: 61

Wins: 56

Losses: 5

Knockouts: 37

YOUR TOP TEN!

In this book, we listed our Top 10 athletes, but not in order. We gave you some facts and information about each of them. Now it's your turn to put the athletes in order. Find a pen and paper. Now make your own list! Who should be No. 1? How about your other nine choices? Would they be the same as ours? Would they be in the same order as they are in this book? Are any athletes missing from this book? Who would you include? It's your call!

Remember, there are no wrong answers. Every fan might have different choices in a different order. Every fan should be able to back up their choices, though. If you need more information, go online and learn. Or find other books about these great players. Then discuss the choices with your friends!

THINK ABOUT THIS . . .

Here are some things to think about when making your own Top 10 list:

- How did each player succeed?
- How important were the championships or events they won?
- Did the athlete help change their sport?
- How did the athlete deal with racism or injustice?

SPORTS GLOSSARY

Big Ten (BIG TEN) a college sports conference located mostly in the Midwest

civilian (siv-IL-yan) anyone who is not part of a nation's military

freshman (FRESH-munn) a person in their first year of high school or college

Grand Slam (GRAND SLAM) in tennis, the four major tournaments—U.S., Australian, and French Opens, and Wimbledon

heptathlon (hepp-TATH-lon) a track event, usually for women, that includes seven running, jumping, and throwing contests over two days

mourned (MORNED) felt sad about someone's death

Negro Leagues (NEE-grow LEEGS) pro baseball groups created for African Americans; the leagues played from the early 1900s into the 1950s

Parkinson's disease (PARK-in-sunz dih-ZEEZ) a serious illness of the brain that affects a person's movement, speech, and body systems

segregated (SEGG-ruh-gay-ted) deliberately separated by race

FIND OUT MORE

IN THE LIBRARY

Buckley, James Jr. *Who Are Venus and Serena Williams?* New York, NY: Penguin/Grosset & Dunlap, 2017.

Buckley, James Jr. *Who Was Jesse Owens?* New York, NY: Penguin/Grosset & Dunlap, 2016.

Doeden, Matt. *Muhammad Ali: The Greatest.* Minneapolis, MN: Lerner/Gateway, 2017.

ON THE WEB

Visit our Web site for links about Top 10 African American athletes: **childsworld.com/links**

Note to Parents, Teachers, and Librarians: We routinely verify our Web links to make sure they are safe and active sites. So encourage your readers to check them out!

INDEX

ABOUT THE AUTHOR

K. C. Kelley has been an editor and writer for *Sports Illustrated* and the National Football League. He has written more than 150 books for young readers. He has written biographies of Ali, Owens, Venus and Serena Williams, Robinson, Roberto Clemente, and many other sports heroes. He lives in Santa Barbara, California.